Published by the National Museums of Scotland
Chambers Street, Edinburgh EH1 1JF

ISBN 0948636 66 1

© John Burnett and the Trustees of the National
Museums of Scotland 1995

British Library Cataloguing in Publication Data

A catalogue record for this book is available for the
British Library

Series editor Iseabail Macleod
Picture research Susan Irvine
Designed and produced by the Publications Office of
the National Museums of Scotland
Printed by Ritchie of Edinburgh

The author is grateful to all those who helped him in many ways, including
Peter Bourhill, Marguerita Burnett, George Dalgleish, Andrew Jackson,
Iseabail Macleod, the staff of the Scottish Ethnological Archives, and Robin
Urquhart.

Acknowledgements

Front cover, 50: Scottish National Portrait Gallery. 4, v (top), vii (top and bottom),
57, 62, 78: Scottish Sports Council. 6, 14, 16, 19, 22, 28, 36, v (bottom), 42, 46, 49,
51, 53, 58, Back cover: National Museums of Scotland. 9: British Library. 12:
Dumfries Museum (Nithsdale District Council). 18: From a Private Collection.
20: J D M Robertson, Shorelands, Kirkwall. 27: Strathclyde Regional Archive. 30,
viii (bottom): John Burnett. 35: Studio Seven. 39: Hugh Cheape, NMS. i (top):
The Earl Cathcart. i (bottom): In the collection of the Stirlings of Keir. ii (top), iii:
City of Edinburgh Art Centre. ii (bottom): Board of Trustees of the National
Museums and Galleries on Merseyside (Walker Art Gallery, Liverpool). iv (top):
Delvine Curling Club. iv (bottom): Reproduced by kind permission ©
Manchester City Art Galleries. vi (top): Royal Highland Agricultural Society. vi
(bottom), 74: Courtesy of George Dalgleish. viii (top): By kind permission of
Kerry Gordon. 44: The Scotsman Publications. 45, 66, 73 (bottom): Trustees of
the National Library of Scotland. 54: Copyright British Museum. 64: Star Photos.
70: Ishbel MacJean. 73 (top): Courtesy of Ian Fleming.

Illustrations captioned SEA are from the Scottish Ethnological Archive in the
National Museums of Scotland.

Front cover: *Golf links at St Andrews in 1847: a detail from
an oil sketch for Charles Lees' painting (see also page 50)*

Back cover: *Hunters with hounds and hawks: detail of a late
eighteenth-century Scots powder horn.*

CONTENTS

INTRODUCTION

Let rogues and let fools
Rin to cards and to dice,
And gamblin, sit girnin and gurlin,   *complaining and growling*
But honest men ken
That tho' slipp'ry the ice
Still fair-play an' fun gang wi' Curlin.

Fair-play and fun: the essence of sport. These lines were written by Sir Alexander Boswell (1775-1822), son of Dr Johnson's biographer, and engraved on a medal of the Curling Society of Kirkconnel in Dumfriesshire. In the nineteenth century curling was by far the most widely played sport in Scotland. It was distinctively Scots: no one else curled. Unlike boxing or horse-racing, it had never been linked with gambling. Indeed, many ministers were keen curlers, including the Reverend John Kerr of Dirleton in East Lothian, the great historian of the game. Boswell's verse is moral, about the right way to behave. Perhaps this is Calvinism on the curling pond, with virtue its own reward, and dinnae girn. Laird and labourer played alongside the minister: sport brought together people of all kinds, though in Victorian Scotland women curlers were rare.

This book is about the history of sport in Scotland, but it is not merely about sport. Its subject is sport as a part of the life of the people, not an isolated experience but an activity which was shaped by patterns of wealth, poverty, leisure and communication, patterns which changed with time. It is concerned also with

Football from the cradle to the grave: 'Maryhill Magyars' by Farquhar McKechnie (1978).

memory, for the events which we remember and the ways that traditions are created and live, are all part of sport. It is, finally, about individual human beings with tired muscles, sore feet, and work to do in the morning.

Duddingston Curling Society badge, 1802.
This is the oldest curling badge. Curling was
the most popular sport in Scotland in the
century before the rise of football in the 1870s.

SPORTING SCOTLAND

1 Kings, queens, burghers, people

King James IV is the first Scot we can name who loved a range of sports; indeed, he enjoyed every sport that was played in Scotland during his reign from 1488 to 1513. Scotland had a cosmopolitan court, bound to Europe by the Christian religion and the Latin tongue. The king himself spoke six languages. Like the royalty and aristocracy of Europe, James IV indulged in the diversions of chivalry, 'tryumphand tournayis, justyng, and knichtly game.' After his wedding to Margaret Tudor, daughter of Henry VII of England, there were three days of jousting and other warlike sports in the courtyard at Holyrood, and James joined in. There was a political point: he wanted his visitors to see that he was personally brave and had all the skills of war. Some say he was overconfident, for he was killed fighting the English at Flodden. His son, James V, was only an infant at the time of the battle in 1513. He married Princess Madeleine in Paris on New Year's Day 1537, and that Renaissance roughneck, François I, became his father-in-law. The wedding was enveloped in jousting and tournaments, and young James went to the altar with a bruised face. He returned home to enlarge and embellish his palaces in the French style. Madeleine died after a few months, but James married another Frenchwoman, Mary of Guise, and the enthusiasm for things French remained. A real tennis court was built at Falkland: it is the oldest building in Scotland erected for sport.

Hawking was the favourite sport of James IV. He paid high prices for birds and was generous to those who gave them to him. He sent falconers to find hawks in remote areas, to bring them back to the mews at Craigforth and Inchkeith. One of the few portraits of him shows a peregrine falcon on his wrist. He enjoyed shooting too, with longbow, crossbow or the comparatively new and explosive hand-culverin: gunpowder and its benefits had reached Scotland in the fifteenth century. There is a vivid story of James, along with burgesses and canons - of the church - from Pittenweem on the Fife coast, bobbing round the Isle of May, firing at the sea birds with culverins.

James was also a golfer. Is golf Scots or Dutch? A game called 'colf' was being played in the Low Countries before golf is recorded in Scotland. It was played both on ice and on dry land, and it can be seen in many paintings. Clubs like golf clubs were used, and the targets were raised from the ground: a hole in the ice would hardly have been suitable. In Scotland, though, a poorer country, fewer documents were written and there are almost no pictures of ordinary life. Whatever was happening in Scotland is unknown to us. If golf came to Scotland from the Netherlands, why did it not appear in East Anglia or on the Lincolnshire coast? Colf seems to have been closer to putting than to the longer game of golf: they are probably not the same sport, though closely related. And it was golf that James played, buying his clubs for a shilling and balls for four pence each.

James IV is the first known Scottish football supporter. The Scottish people had been so much given to football that it had been prohibited by a number of Acts of Parliament, starting in 1424; in 1457 football and golf were banned because they were so popular that they took attention from archery. James, however, was an enthusiast. In 1497 the Lord Treasurer, who looked after his money, paid two shillings 'to buy fut balles to the King in Stirling'.

The first notice of horse racing at Leith, later to become so popular, dates from James's reign. A payment was made in 1504 to 'the boy that ran the King's horse' at Leith, the jockey. Soon a poet would write:

And sum, to schaw thare courtlie corsis,
Wald ryid to Leith, and ryn thare horssis,
And wychtlie wallope ouer the sandis.   vigorously

8

James himself was a tireless horseman who once rode from Stirling to Aberdeen, and on to Elgin, 180 miles in a day. He was an active man and enjoyed vigorous games, such as long bowls, in which the length of the throw was more important than accuracy.

King David I (1084-1153) surrounded by his huntsmen, horses and hounds in the Miracle of the Holy Rood by Malcolm Ramsay, 1486.

He also played caitch or cache-pule, the French *jeu de paume* of which real tennis is a more sophisticated form. The Lord Treasurer's accounts contain payments because 'The King played at the caitch and tynt [lost] ...'.

James V was only 30 years old when he died in 1542. The decline in his health probably began with a hunting accident at Stirling. In the fifteenth and sixteenth centuries hunting was the main sport of royalty and of the aristocracy. The usual method was the chasing of animals by dogs. James V was in Atholl in 1528 in pursuit of red deer, roe deer, wolves, foxes and wild cats. When Mary, Queen of Scots hunted there in 1564 deer were herded from all over the Grampians towards Glen Tilt for two months before her arrival. On the day, 360 were driven towards the royal party and killed by dogs. In some cases, hunting was the pursuit of troublesome vermin. In Mary's reign fear of wolves was so great that they were said to dig up human corpses, and no doubt they did severe damage to livestock. Wolves were pursued into extinction in Scotland in the eighteenth century.

James VI has been given the character of a scholar and pedant, and he was certainly timid in many things. But he was also a horseman almost without fear, and he had a passion - no lesser word will do - for hunting. He thought the stag the monarch not just of the glen but of the whole animal kingdom. 'He seems to have forgotten that he is a King, except in the pursuit of stags, to which he is quite devoted', said the Venetian ambassador to London. After his dogs had killed an animal, James would cut its throat, slit its belly and then with his own bloody hands daub the faces of his courtiers to show his regard for their sportsmanship. He also took pleasure in cock-fighting and bear-bating.

Horse-racing spread in the time of James VI. At Dumfries in 1575

> my Lord Hamilton had a horse so well bridled, and so speedy, that although he was of a meaner stature from other horses that essayed their speed, he overcame them all upon Solway sands, whereby he obtained great praise both of England and Scotland.

James set up the course at Newmarket and imported Arab horses, improving the breeding stock. The whole of Britain benefited, and more Scots burghs set up annual races. The oldest Scottish racing trophy is the Lanark Bell, dating from the first decade of the seventeenth century. The race for the Bell was last run in 1977, but it may be revived. Other races began at the same time at Paisley (1608), Dunfermline (by 1610), Perth (1613), Cupar (1621), and Jedburgh (1625). There must have been more.

So far we have been discussing the sport of the upper classes. What about the common people? There is a real difficulty in knowing what sports were followed: lack of evidence. Field football was played over all over Europe, and though it only crops up occasionally in Scottish texts, it was probably widespread. In criticizing the clergy for spending too much time at leisure, the poet had an abbot boast

> I wot there is nocht ane among you all
> More finelie can play at the fute-ball.

Many would follow the monarch's example as far as they could. We know that caitch, for example, was being played at Lanark in 1570, but only because of a legal case over the ownership of a sword. One of the disputants said that he had made a bargain when he was 'coming from the caitche'. It seems that among ordinary people the most usual form of caitch was played against a wall, with balls of the kind that are preserved at Arbroath Abbey: wool packed tight inside a leather or wool covering. In various forms this game was played all over Europe. It survives, in a simple form of handball, in Ireland; the Basques play pelota in a number of more complex variants, usually using a wicker extension to the arm to throw the ball further and faster. Using rackets and standard courts it became fives and then squash. A good description of it as 'handy' was written in 1870, when caitch was dying out in Scotland. There were two teams, each of six or eight or ten.

> The game was for one man of each team alternately to strike the
> ball back to the wall with his hand, and the side which first failed

to send it back lost one, which the other gained. And don't run away with the idea this was the innocent play this looks on paper. There were creases right and left perpendicularly, and above and below horizontally outside which the ball could not strike to count. There were clever fellows who could make it rebound from the wall thirty or forty feet as neatly as if cut; and there were sometimes cleverer ones who could send it back all that distance low enough to touch the wall just inside the lower crease. Men stripped to the work, and rolled up their shirt sleeves on their stout arms, and swung and sweat over it to a discipline as exacting as anything which prevails on the cricket-field or amongst football players; to be the best handy player of a district was to be a hero.

Handball continued in Ayrshire: an annual meeting was held at Galston on the Saturday of Glasgow Fair until the Second World War. At Galston it was played against the wall of Barr Castle - 'Baur Alley' - the wall being of the fifteenth century, and the game of the same period.

Caitch was played for pleasure, but archery was a sport with a military purpose. The medieval prohibitions on football and golf

The Dumfries siller gun, 1617.

had been matched by a requirement to build butts and have regular archery practice after church on Sunday: all adult men were expected to take part. The Scots archers had never had the numbers or skill of their English counterparts, as had been painfully shown at Homildon Hill, Flodden and other disastrous battles, so the practice was needed.

With time, technology moved forward. James VI tried to shift interest to training in the use of firearms, and gave to the burgh of Kirkcudbright in 1587 and Dumfries about 1617, miniature silver guns as prizes for shooting competitions. The Kirkcudbright siller gun is the oldest sporting trophy in Scotland. Archery was still enjoyed, however, partly because longbows and crossbows were still used in hunting. The bow was still a weapon. The last battle in which archers had a large role was between the Camerons and the MacIntoshes about 1664: in 1676 Britain's oldest archery society was founded in Edinburgh, the Royal Company of Archers. Significantly, it was not for the common man, but for those with leisure.

2 Decline and revival

When travelling from Edinburgh to London in 1617 James VI found that in Lancashire the Puritans were preventing sport after the church service on Sunday. He supported the country people who had complained, not so much because of love of sport as because he wanted to lessen the political power of the Puritans. James had the Bishop of Chester write *A Declaration of Sports* in his name, attacking the ban:

> For when shal the common people have leave to exercise, if not upon the Sundayes and Holydayes, seeing they must apply their labour, and winne their living in all working dayes?

Here we have sport as a political football. The *Declaration* was published in England, but in Scotland at the same period sport on Sunday, in other words sport itself, was similarly under attack for religious reasons. There is no doubt that around this time the amount of sport decreased:

> Manly exercise is shrewdly gone,
> Football and wrestling, throwing of the stone;
> Jumping and breathing, practices of strength
> Which taught them to endure hard things at length.

'Breathing' refers to contests in which people tried to hold their breath for the longest time.

Cromwell, whose period of complete power in Scotland began in 1650, forbade sport, but the tide soon turned. In May 1660 Charles II landed at Dover, and by the following year advertisements like this were appearing:

> The famous horse race of Coupar, in Fife, which by the iniquity of the times hath been so long buried, to the great dissatisfaction of our nobility and gentry, is to be run upon the second Tuesday in April.

At Leith there was racing every Saturday. The upsurge of interest in sport among the gentry was partly a reaction against Puritan

The Stirling burgh prize for archery, 1698. The prize was probably a sum of money to be put towards a piece of silver and William Dundas chose this box and its engraving.

discipline, and partly due to the court making gambling fashionable. Large sums were staked on horses and in the new cockpit at Leith. All over the country, a wide range of sporting activity reappeared. General Tam Dalyell, a staunch royalist who had been in exile with Charles II, died in 1685. In the inventory of his house in West Lothian, the Binns, there were in the saddle house swords and bullet moulds - he pursued the Covenanters with vigour - and also curling stones of stone, iron and wood.

Sir John Foulis of Ravelston had his country house three miles west of Edinburgh. There he enjoyed country sports: hare coursing, fishing and hawking. He lived close enough to Leith - then, and for years after, the sporting capital of Scotland - to watch the horse racing and play golf. He was a keen golfer: his account books show payments for wagers he lost; and in the evening he played cards for small sums. His ledgers show a payment in 1672 for a golf club for his son Archie, and thirty-five years later for a club and balls for two of his grandsons. He gave a football to another son in 1691. Sir John was also a bowler. There is no reason to suppose that his sporting was anything other than typical of a Scots laird of the period. What is unusual is the survival of his accounts, which reveal his daily life.

Shooting the papingo or popinjay at Kilwinning was one of the more unusual sports which were revived at the Restoration. Shooting the popinjay was also practised in the Low Countries and Germany, and it is said to stem from an incident in Vergil's *Aeneid*. Aeneas is in Sicily where he finds archers shooting at a tethered dove. One misses, but breaks the bindings holding the bird, then to quote the translation (about 1513) by Gavin Douglas, Bishop of Dunkeld:

> With arow reddy nokkyt than Ewricion
> Plukkis vp inhy hys bow ...
> Hys arow he threw vnder the clowdis blak,
> And persyt hir quyte owtthrou the bak;
> Hyr lyfe sche lost heich vp in the ayr.

At Kilwinning the object was for an archer to knock a wooden parrot off the top of the Abbey. The competition was said to have begun in the reign of James IV, and it was certainly restored to life in 1688. We will meet it again in a later chapter.

3 The eighteenth century

It is only after the first Jacobite rising that frequent accounts of the sporting activities of ordinary people are to be found. A surprising amount of sporting poetry was written. Rather than give an account of the development of golf, horse racing and the rest, based on a patchwork of sources which historians have only partly stitched together, here is a short anthology of poetry arising from six sports, which conveys what few had revealed before - that sport was fun, part of a healthy society in which people came together to enjoy themselves.

Horse racing and most other competitions were annual events which played a large part in shaping the peoples' year. John

'Coming from the races' by Walter Geikie (1795-1837). The Saturday of Leith races was followed by notoriously heavy drinking.

Mayne (1759-1836) wrote *The Siller Gun* about the shooting for the gun at Dumfries:

> For weeks before this fête sae clever,
> The fowk were in a perfect fever,
> Scouring gun-barrels i' the river -
>   At marks practizing -
> Marching wi' drums and fifes for ever -
>   A' sodgerizing!
>
> And turning coats, and mending breeks,
> New-seating where the sark-tail keeks;   shirt-tail peeps out
> (Nae matter tho' the cloot that eeks
>   Is black or blue;)
> And darning, with a thousand steeks,   stitches
>   The stockings too.

As for the preparations on the day of the event, the Edinburgh poet Robert Fergusson (1750-74) described all the excitement of Leith Races: the Town Guard dressing up in their best uniforms, and even shaving, the procession behind the Town's Purse, one of the prizes, which was carried on top of a pole, and the visitors from outside Edinburgh. Leith Races was Scotland's biggest sporting gathering. The crowd is said to have been 20,000 strong by 1790. Boys would go through the old town in Fergusson's time - the New Town had yet to be built - selling handbills -

> 'Here is the true and faithfu' list
> 'O' noblemen and horses;
> 'Their eild, their weight, their height,   age
>   their grist,
> 'That rin for plates or purses
>   'Fu' fleet this day.'

The day ended with a free fight in the streets of Leith.

Allan Ramsay (c.1685-1758) was a milder man than Robert Fergusson, more gentle and more genteel. One can imagine Fergusson joining in the rammy at Leith: Ramsay would have been talking about it in a howff. He was admitted a member of the

James, 5th Earl of Wemyss, in the uniform of the Royal Company of Archers, about 1715.

Royal Company of Archers in 1724, and went respectably with them for a day's shooting.

> While, to gain sport and hailsome air,
> The blythsome spirit draps dull care,
>   And starts frae bus'ness free:
> Now to the fields the Archers bend,
> With friendly minds the day to spend,
>   In manly game and glee.

In another poem Ramsay pictures a club spending an evening sociably together. The members are no longer out of doors:

> Driving their ba's frae whin or tee
> There's no ae gouffer to be seen
> Nor doucer folk wysin a-jee   [aiming with a sideways turn]
> The byas bowls on Tamson's green.

Thomson's bowling green was in the Cowgate, one of several in the city.

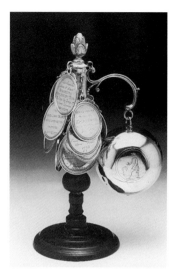

The Silver Jack of the Edinburgh Society of Bowlers, or 'Societatis Sphaerastrum', 1771, with medals added by twelve winners.

Alexander Pennecuik (1652-1722), a physician and friend of Ramsay, was also a poet. He wrote of a sport that was steadily growing:

> To Curle on the Ice, does greatly please,
> Being a manly Scotish Exercise;
> It Clears the Brains, stirs up the Native Heat,
> And gives a gallant Appetite for Meat.

The most violent and colourful language is to be found in *The Christmas Bawing of Monymusk*. This is a description of an annual football match, a match almost without rules, written in 1739. The author was John Skinner (1721-1807), who was at the time schoolmaster at Monymusk near Aberdeen. As soon as the match begins

They yowph'd the ba' frae dyke to dyke	struck
Wi' unco speed and virr.	vigour

After thirty stanzas of cheerful thuggery

> Jock Jalop shouted like a gun,
> As something had him ail'd,
> 'Fy sirs', quo' he, 'the bonspale's win,   game
> And we the ba' have hail'd.

In other words, a goal has been scored by carrying the ball over a line, the 'hail'. The game was over. The players then threw themselves on the ground and get out their 'snishin-millies', their snuff mulls, and decide to take their thirst to an inn. The poem shows football involving the whole village: the watchers are expected to take part in the play from time to time. In a few places 'ba' games' of this kind went on until the twentieth century, and they are still held in the Borders at Jedburgh and in Orkney at Kirkwall.

The Ba' game at Kirkwall, Orkney, on Christmas Day, 1955, a surviving cousin of the football at Monymusk. SEA

Lastly Robert Burns (1759-96), who wrote an elegy on his friend Tam Samson of Kilmarnock, an addict of many sports.

> That woefu' morn be ever mourn'd,
> Saw him in shootin graith adorn'd,   gear
> While pointers round impatient burn'd,
>   Frae couples free'd;
> But, och! he gae'd and ne'er returned!
>   Tam Samson's deid!

The 'pointers' were the dogs which were used to flush out the game, as the sportsman walked the fields, unlike the modern practice of beaters driving grouse towards static guns. The same poem contains the most famous lines of Scottish sporting verse - to curlers at least:

> He was the king o' a' the core,
> To guard, or draw, or wick a bore,
> Or up the rink like Jehu roar,
>   In time o' need;
> But now he lags on Death's 'hog-score' -
>   Tam Samson's deid!

4 Clubs

Sport is a social activity. The people who play sport also engage in other social activities, and sport reflects them. We have already seen archery move from war to leisure. The very fact that sport brought people together meant that while they were meeting they did other things. In the sixteenth century Border reivers went to horse races to plan their raids to 'lift' cattle. At Huntly the horse race held irregularly between 1695 and 1749 was a cover for a Jacobite gathering. The entry money went to the poor - provided they prayed for the Pretender.

Sports meetings were also social gatherings in the broadest sense. There was talking, eating and drinking. Clubs for dining and drinking grew up in the larger burghs in the eighteenth century. A club would meet in a particular tavern, foreshadowing their own club house. Some linked themselves with a particular sport. At the same time, there began to be an advantage to sportsmen in having control of the facilities they needed, the patch of land for a golf course, or a club house, bowl house or meeting hall. The first sporting club in Scotland was the Company of Archers, founded in 1676; they built Archers' Hall in 1776-7, which they still use. It is no accident that it is beside Edinburgh's oldest surviving bowling green. The Duddingston Curling Club dates from 1795: their house beside Duddingston Loch, a mock-medieval tower, was put up in 1825. The oldest golf club is the Honourable Society of Edinburgh Golfers (1744), who initially played on Leith Links. Within a few decades they had dozens of imitations, including the Royal and Ancient at St Andrews (1754), later to become the ruling body of golf.

Clubs were not founded merely for sport. The social side was equally important: long dinners and heavy drinking. It has been

Scott, himself a golfer, knew the game's ancient history, and his feeling for sport was the same as J Ewbank's in this engraving (1825). It was the present living amidst the past.

suggested that many of the eighteenth-century golf clubs were Masonic Lodges: members were obliged to dine, required to wear uniforms, and were initiated into secret mysteries, and women were rigorously excluded. Does this add up to Masonry, or was the Lodge the only model for what a club might be? The Bruntsfield Golf Club in Edinburgh bought aprons and caps in 1801, but what happened elsewhere? It is at least certain that golf clubs were for far more than sport, and this carried golf through a lean period in the late eighteenth and early nineteenth centuries when it might otherwise have died - the fate of similar sports in the Netherlands.

5 The medieval revival

Scotland was at the heart of the Industrial Revolution: Carron ironworks opened on the shores of the Forth in 1759, and James Watt was in Glasgow when he made the decisive improvements to the steam engine in 1763/4. There was more haste, noise and soot. As Britain puffed and clattered towards the future, some people looked back to the Middle Ages, wishing vainly for the stable society they could see, or imagine, there.

Sir Walter Scott (1771-1832) was the leading medievalist. He was the first novelist whose works sold on a huge scale, and he created a popular interest in history, and a knowledge and under-standing of it. He reinforced his writing with historical pageants, particularly the ones which involved in the visit of King George IV to Edinburgh in 1822. He encouraged the wearing of tartan because he saw it as the old, and thus the best, way of dressing. He built Abbotsford in Gothic style. Despite being lame from childhood, Scott loved sport, and supported sporting clubs with enthusiasm. The Six-Feet Club was a group of Edinburgh pro-fessional men whose name stated the chief qualification for membership: they met for 'fencing, single-stick, throwing the hammer, tossing the bar, putting the stone, quoits, running, leaping, rifle shooting, goff, curling, &c'. Scott was their 'Umpire of the games, who has been elected for life', and they emphasized their interest in the past by becoming the Guard of Honour to the Hereditary High Constable of Scotland.

James Hogg (1770-1835), 'The Ettrick Shepherd', shared Scott's liking for sport, and was even more active. A man of great enthusiasms, he threw himself into every kind of country sport - running, jumping, fishing, wrestling, quoiting, curling, archery - and excelled at them. In 1827 he organized 'Border Games' at Innerleithen in the Tweed valley: they were, and are still, held annually. The games of 1829 were described in verse, revealing Hogg at his most ebullient, the centre of the activity, organizing a foot race.

'Stand back!' baw'ld Hogg; 'Once! - Constables, I say,
Keep the crowd back - Twice! - Odd! we canna see -
Clear the course - Brodie, gar your baton play -   make
That'll do fine - noo tak a breath awee -
Twice! - O! ye deevils, fast! rin! rin away!
They're oot o'sight already! back to me,
My hearties! - glorious! round the pole! they leave it!
Well done, Rob Laidlaw! - in, in! - Lord, ye have it!

Hogg and Scott were, in political terms, Tories. They lived in a period of radical agitation and low prices for the produce of the land, and they saw the people of Scotland becoming poorer and more unhappy. Their response was to seek better ways of life in the past, and a part of this was the re-creation of ancient sports. They were both present at a revival of a football match at Carterhaugh near Selkirk in 1815. Scott praised archery in various places in his poetry and novels, most vividly in *Ivanhoe* (1820), in which one of the leading characters, Locksley, is in fact Robin Hood. The Games at Innerleithen included an archery competition. The prize was a silver arrow modelled on the Musselburgh Arrow of 1713, and an accurate replica of the arrows which were used in the contest, and of those which had been shot in battles five hundred years before.

One of the readers of *Ivanhoe* was the Earl of Eglinton. He was even more of a Tory than Scott, deeply aware of his aristocratic ancestry. When the coronation of Queen Victoria was celebrated with the minimum of pomp and ceremony he was disgusted, and decided to re-create a medieval tournament, complete with knights jousting, to demonstrate that tradition and pageantry still had a place in the life of the nation. The result was comic. One hundred thousand people from all over Britain travelled to Ayrshire and assembled at Eglinton Castle near Irvine, and were drenched in rain which turned the ground of the Lists to a liquid in which the tilting, quintain and hand-to-hand combat took place. The tournament had to be curtailed. In the confusion the 'swell mob', well-dressed London pickpockets, profited greatly, and the Earl became fabulously in debt to his bankers.

His bankers, however, were content to lend money to an Earl whose real wealth was in coal: for all his medieval tastes, much of his income came from mining and the iron industry. The revival of chivalry was partly a reaction against the intrusion of pit head-stocks and villages built for miners' families on the margins of the Eglinton estate. Another laird who recoiled from progress in the same way was Alastair Macdonnell of Glengarry. The famous portrait by Raeburn shows him in recently re-invented Highland dress, with his sporting rifle in his hand. He extracted huge payments from the builders of the Caledonian Canal, which crossed his land in the Great Glen, revived various sports and was one of the early proponents of Highland Games.

The Kilwinning papingo has already been mentioned. Eglinton supported it, and the Irvine Archers too - in fact, he took them over. Irvine and Kilwinning were beside Eglinton Castle, and were another outlet for his medieval fantasies. The Irvine archers formed the guard of honour for the Queen of Beauty at the Tournament, and from 1840 the Irvine meeting was said to commemorate the Tournament's anniversary. There were uniforms and paternalism. The Kilwinning competition still had a local flavour, and when it was over the archers marched to the cross where the Captain danced a reel with an elderly woman named Tibbie Glen. She outlived the competition, which lost its popularity after the Earl's death. It was revived after the Second World War.

The fascination of the history of sport is the discovery of the range of roles it can play in society, and the ways it has been used at various times to promote one view or another of society. Tories like Scott and Eglinton saw sport as a way of keeping people happy. A writer in the *Ayr Advertiser* in 1841 tried to start a 'National Games of Scotland' which would be held on New Year's Day, to

> substitute innocent sports for the unmeaning dissipation which but too often takes place on New Year's Day.

This was not disinterested patronage: it was an attempt to take control of the people's leisure. Eglinton's enthusiasm for the Middle Ages included a wish for an Ayrshire in which an Earl stood unchallenged at the top of the social heap and everyone else knew their place. He was a Conservative and a conservative, deeply unhappy at the idea of change. He hoped sport would distract the working classes from radical politics.

A radical might take entirely the opposite view to Eglinton, and condemn sport. The largest games in Fife in the 1850s were at Thornton. The *Fifeshire Advertiser* said:

> It is very questionable if these games are to be compared with the cheap trips to the large cities. The benefit derived from a day spent amid the magnificence of architecture and the glories of monumental sculpture is indeed far beyond the viewing of, or joining in, those rude feats of strength and agility which belong to a darker age, and with which out modern Thorntonians are so much delighted.

Cultivating the mind, the writer says, is to be preferred to exercising the body, and manual labourers and their families need education before amusement.

Games like the ones at Thornton had mixtures of sports which show evidence of the medieval revival, of the revived existing beside the new. For example, there was a meeting of the County Archery and Rifle Club at Linlithgow in 1849. They copied the Kilwinning papingo: a wooden parrot was shot off the

*Ticket for the Captain-General's ball, Kilwinning, August
1846. Lord Eglinton was, of course, the Captain-General.
The scene of the medieval fantasy is Kilwinning Abbey, with
Eglinton Castle in the distance.*

south-west tower of the Palace. There were also rifle competitions. Ten years later the Grand National Games were held at
Wishaw. Some of it was ancient: tilting at the ring on horseback,
just like the Bonnie Earl of Moray. Some of it was Scottish:
tossing the caber, piping, the sword dance. There were races and
jumping contests of all kinds. Last, there was climbing the greasy
pole for a leg of mutton, which had appealed for centuries to
crowds all over Europe, and like other crowds before it the one at
Wishaw brought down the pole and filched the mutton before a
winner had been found.

So far we have been looking at the deliberate copying of the
Middle Ages. The sports of ordinary people included games

which had continued from year to year for - how long? This was written of Hamilton in the first half of the nineteenth century:

> The boys, instead of being confined, like those of the larger manufacturing towns, in unhealthy cotton mills, are permitted ... to play at the ba' and shinty, or at bows and arrows, or else to roam a field in search of birds' nests. On the haughs in the summer evenings, the young men would be seen 'putting the stane', or playing at 'the pennystanes' [quoits], or perhaps amusing themselves with the more energetic game of football.

King George of Great Britain was on the throne: but perhaps these sports, not the inventions of Scott, Hogg and Eglinton, were the real survivals from the time when King James stood at the head of the Scottish nation.

Climbing the greasy pole at the Ferry Fair, South Queensferry, 1950s: an ancient competition in an ancient burgh.
SEA

6 The community and the sportsman

Many sports have died out. Some of them expired because of social pressure: the sport became seen by the community as a whole as being too violent or too cruel, so the sportsman changed his behaviour. This created an opportunity for new sports to grow, particularly at a time when everyone's lives were being reshaped by the opening of railways and the possibilities they brought for travel.

Prize fighting - bare knuckle boxing with some wrestling throws allowed - never had the popularity in Scotland which it enjoyed in England. It was illegal but flourished because it was supported by royalty. As the nineteenth century progressed the growing police forces became adept at preventing it. Sandy M'Kay, the Scottish champion, died in 1830 after a fight in England: his opponent was tried for murder. 'Another of these blackguard and degrading exhibitions,' said the *Scotsman*. One of the last prize fighters was John Docherty (1844-1904). We know a little about him from the Glasgow Poor Law Records: Docherty died in poverty. His last fight should have been at Provanmill bridge, but the police arrived before it started. The party rushed in cabs along Lambhill bridge, further along the Forth and Clyde Canal. The police arrested Docherty after the fight, and prize fighting was at its sleazy end.

A sign of changing attitudes was the founding in 1824 of the Society for the Prevention of Cruelty to Animals. Cockfighting had been a traditional sport on Fastern's E'en (Shrove Tuesday), or in some places on the first Monday in the New Year, Hansel Monday. Boys brought cocks to school, where the fights were held and the schoolmaster kept the dead animals and the 'fugies' - birds which refused to fight. In the second half of the eighteenth century the sport had begun to fall out of favour, and it had all but vanished from schools by the 1840s. In West Lothian the cocks were entered in the boys' names but in fact belonged to adults who bet on the results. 'This is a most degrading and brutal pastime, and should not be permitted by the authorities' (1848).

Cockfighting then went underground, and continued its modest and vicious existence well in to the twentieth century.

The cat race was recorded at St Andrews and Haddington. It was not a race as such: men on horseback struck with a hammer a barrel suspended above them. When the end was knocked out the cat fell out of the barrel and was caught by the tail by one of the crowd who threw it in the air: this was repeated until the cat was dead. At Haddington there was soot in the barrel which blinded the cat and made it less able to escape. Even more barbaric was the goose race. The fullest account is of the event at St Andrews, though other burghs were just as guilty. A live goose was tied up by the legs, its neck having been plucked bare and its neck greased. Horsemen tried to take off the bird's head while it writhed.

Cart and plough horses were raced all over Scotland, but in the Lothians there was a concentration of popular festivals, carters' plays, which involved the whole working-class community. The

play day would begin with a procession to the race ground, usually a stretch of road. Thomas Watson, a gardener in Lasswade, has given us a picture of a horse entered for the race:

> While there's a horse frae Kevock-Mill,
> I think they ca' him Bassy,
> And on his side I'll lay a gill
> A better ne'er trod causey.
> Some sax saddles he has took -
> An unco beast for winning;
> Baith at Lasswade and Penicuik
> His name is famed for rinning
> On their play-day.

Jamie Hendry of the Newton-on-Ayr Whipmen, one of the last survivors of the carters' society which raced its horses on the sands.

The prizes were practical: saddles, bridles, even bootlaces. There was no landed patron, no silverware. This was typical of popular sport. At Aberdeen in 1766 it was advertised

> that there are two races to be run for men; the first for a piece of English cloth for a coat, a bonnet, and a pair of shoes; the second for 10/-. And two races for women, the first for a piece of check for a gown, some yards of linen, and a silk napkin; the second for 10/-. The above prizes are given by the Honourable Company for Water Drinkers at Peterhead.

The prizes did not in themselves mark the superiority of the winner, they just helped with everyday life.

At the Lasswade carters' play there were few rules, but dancing, dinner, drinking and boisterous revelry. Watson ends his poem the morning after:

> But night is bye, and mornin's in;
> There's mony a weary frame,
> Ere these queer bodies do begin
> To tak' the road they came.
> When they get hame, they then, nae doubt,
> Amang the blankets creep,
> And there at last they ha'd it out
> Beside auld daddy Sleep
> Their friend that morn.

The carters' plays died out around 1860, though the ones at Gilmerton and West Linton survived by losing their riotous element. Society was becoming more controlled, more disciplined. This was one of the reasons for the ending of Leith races, transferred to Musselburgh in 1816. Alexander Campbell lamented that

> the Musselburgh races are utterly and wholly destitute of any portion of that reckless and thorough-going spirit of hilarity, which never failed to attend those of Leith. The former ... are the coldest and most heartless things imaginable; and what they have gained in elegance and refinement, but indifferently supplies the

place of the obstreperous interest, which the rough and round skelping on the plashy sands of Leith was wont to excite.

What was a riot to one was a whole-hearted revel to another. Traditional sports died as Britain adopted values which we now call Victorian.

The Kipper Fair at Newton-on-Ayr was similar to the carters' plays. Although the burgh faced Ayr across the river, it was proud of its independent traditions. This festival celebrated the end of the salmon fishing season, though by 1830 the carters moved all sorts of goods to and from Ayr harbour, and not salmon. The Burgh of Newton supported the horse racing on the sands by offering the prize of a saddle. Going to the beach there was a procession of horses and families, and a local pipe or brass band. Everyone was part of the fun. A local printer, 'Treacle Doup' Connell, sold a scurrilous broadsheet lampooning horses and riders. In time, however, the Kipper Fair lost its flavour. There was concern about safety because the Clydesdales would sometimes rush into the crowd, and the course became less attractive after a railway was built along the high-water mark. The races moved inland in 1880, the course was roped, dignity prevailed, and everyone lost interest.

After the horse races at Newton were other entertainments - foot races, including an old wife's race for a pound of tea, and climbing the greasy pole for a leg of mutton. Around 1860 this was won every year by Willie Anderson, otherwise 'Blood'. He was blind, and the boys pushed him upwards with a pole applied to his rump: he blasphemed fluently. The pole would be taken away, and down would come Blood. Finally he was allowed to reach the mutton and took it off for the best meal of his year.

Rather brutal amusement might also be had at a regatta. There were 'thousands upon thousands' at the Royal Forth Regatta at Granton in 1859. After the races for yachts, rowing boats and skiffs, the fisherwomen took to the water.

The irregular dipping and frequent splashing of the oars, the fouling caused by running in each other's course, or by coming in collision with the impertinent intruders that pursued and crossed them, gives to the ladies' vigorous efforts much the same place that a donkey race holds on turf.

The idea that women should take part only in the most restrained sports, such as archery and croquet, was Victorian. Earlier, on Fastern's E'en (Shrove Tuesday) the married women of Musselburgh had played the spinsters at football, and at Lamington in the Clyde valley there was a similar curling match.

The end of some traditional sports was caused by the increase both in the wealth of the people and the cheapness of whisky: strong drink washed over the whole day instead of being limited to the evening. This happened at some of the carters' plays in the Lothians, and at the shooting for the Siller Gun in Dumfries. In 1885 it was said that

> this festival has of late become unpopular, from the number of accidents by which it is characterized. The drinking is never postponed to the termination of sport. The consequence is riot and outrage. A case is recorded of a man having fired when so overcome by liquor that the gun was held for him by his friends, and yet he hit the mark and was declared victor, though he was not aware of his good fortune till next morning.

Certain sports were almost confined to the miners, who were often a group apart from the rest of society. Hainching - hurling a stone or iron ball along a road to see who could reach a defined point in the smallest number of throws - died out but was re-introduced by Irishmen who came to work in the pits in the middle of the nineteenth century. The police tried to stamp it out because it was dangerous, but it finally faded away about 1940 because other sports, and a world war, took the miners' attention. Pigeon racing was chiefly a miners' sport, and so was cock fighting after about 1840.

The club became the representative of the village. Curling, up to the 1840s, was played either between friends or between parishes. Two parishes would agree a date and a venue, a pond or loch which preferably stood on the boundary. When the men had assembled the match was held between all of the men in the smaller group against an equal number drawn from the larger. Ability on the ice was less important than joining in. When both parishes had curling clubs the number of players would be agreed in advance: the club organized but it also excluded, and there was a loss to the parish when some players became spectators only, and had others to represent them.

As teams played opponents from a wider area than merely the next parish, nicknames were invented. These usually gave the village's main trade. In Ayrshire football, for example, Annbank were the Miners, Beith the Cabinet Makers, Girvan the Fishermen, Maybole the Shoemakers and Stevenston Thistle the Dynamitards because of the explosives works at Ardeer.

The railway made it easier to visit places and events - sportsmen and spectators could travel further and more often. The Eglinton Tournament was at the beginning of this change. Many of the crowd came by rail from Ardrossan: trains had been running for only a few weeks. After the opening of the Edinburgh and Glasgow Railway in 1842 east and west were drawn together. Spectators could travel from Edinburgh to Irvine races, and home in a day. The railway network spread rapidly. Suddenly it was possible for curlers to hold Grand Matches between the north and south of Scotland. The first to attract a large attendance was held at Lochwinnoch, between Paisley and Ayr, in 1850. The rink from Penicuik left at 4 a.m. to catch the first train at Edinburgh, and reached the Renfrewshire venue at noon. They were home at midnight, exhausted - but the journey would have been impossible ten years before. Quoiters, too, started to range more widely: almost as soon as the Edinburgh and Northern Railway was opened across Fife, men from Markinch and Burntisland played together for the first time.

One of Eglinton's innovations was the bowling bonspiel for the Eglinton Jug, a competition between Glasgow and Ayrshire clubs. First held in 1857 it was played in alternate years on the greens of Glasgow and Ayrshire: each club went to another, and all the scores were added up. The point is that the bonspiel was held on a single day. The railway moved the players and the electric telegraph calculated the result.

The final effect of the railway was to make it possible to assemble regularly the large crowds needed to feed professional sport, particularly football. This had to be done quickly, on a Saturday afternoon. We will return to football later.

Willie Penman of Larkhall, one of Scotland's great quoiters, at Vale of Leven Quoiting Club, 1957/8. SEA

7 Sports for Victorian men

In Queen Victoria's long reign from 1837 to 1901, Britain developed as a great industrial nation and spread its empire over the globe. So much changed as the population grew, moved from the country into the cities, and left for the colonies and America while others arrived in Scotland, particularly the Irish. Many traditional values were swept away, and the Britain we live in now is still a Victorian country in its ideas about work and leisure. It was in Britain that modern sport was created. For most of the nineteenth century the leading games in Scotland were curling and bowling, and they are given their own section in this book. So let us start in what may seem an unlikely place, with cricket.

Cricket was a popular game in Scotland between 1860 and the First World War. Indeed, for a short period before the rise of football in the 1870s it was probably the most popular team game in Scotland. In England cricket had evolved from a number of pre-existing sports in the eighteenth century. A form of it had been played in parts of Scotland, particularly Perthshire, under the name of 'cat and bat'. Cricket is first known to have been played in Scotland at Schawpark, near Alloa, when several leading figures in the game in England were present. They were noblemen: the year was 1785. By the 1820s cricket was played in Glasgow, Edinburgh, Perth and Stirling. Its expansion afterwards was brought about by Englishmen who came to work north of the Border, in mines and quarries in Galloway, in the

Silver medal of the Newtongrange Lothian Cricket Club for their best batsman of 1887, Thomas Blackie.

Border woollen mills, or as teachers in a variety of towns. The first club in Forres was started by men who were building the railway bridge over the River Findhorn. In the second half of the century almost every town in the Midland valley had at least one club, and in Aberdeenshire the game was very popular. Fraserburgh had five clubs in 1890, Peterhead eleven. Except for the wealthier clubs, however, the play was often of a low standard because of the poor quality of the pitches. 'The fact of Caledonia being stern and wild has long been a matter of congratulation to the poetic child, but it is a constant source of disgust to the cricketer.'

Cricket was the first team game that was widely played in summer, and it acted as the springboard for other team sports. The first international football match was held on a cricket field, Hamilton Crescent, Glasgow, the home of West of Scotland C.C. In Perth, St Johnstone Cricket Club started a football team: it was the football team that survived. The members of Hawick Cricket Club bought a rugby ball to keep themselves fit in winter, and after a while the rugby club separated. A cricket team in Kilmarnock took up rugby, then changed to football. Thus Kilmarnock's football team still play at Rugby Park.

Team games grew in the Victorian era. So did sports which involved racing of one kind or another, but they grew more slowly. Foot and horse races were common at the beginning of the century, but football, cricket, curling and bowls were dominant by its end. After the Napoleonic Wars regattas were highly popular for a generation or two: Nelson was a hero everywhere. The largest events were on the Clyde at Glasgow and Greenock, and on the Forth. Most of the towns on the Firth of Clyde had smaller race days. At Stranraer the Loch Ryan regatta gave status to the town when it was vying with Portpatrick to be the packet station for Ireland. The Burgh of Wigtown promoted a regatta on the Cree estuary - for two years only. The Kirkcudbright regatta was a larger event. Several thousand watched its six rowing races in 1838. There was a silver cup for 'amateurs ... not to be Seamen, Fishermen, Handcraftsmen or Labourers.' Most other regattas included yachting which had been confined to the Thames, the Channel and the south coast of Ireland before 1820: Scotland's first yacht club was the Royal Northern, on the Clyde (1824).

The most common form of racing, however, was the simplest: running. Long races, short races, walking, running, hurdling, running for money or for fun, Scotland was on foot. At the beginning of the nineteenth century the most famous pedestrian, as he was called, was Captain Barclay of Urie, near Stonehaven. He was a landowner and a gambler. In 1800 and 1801 he backed himself to walk 90 miles in 21½ hours: once he could not start because he was ill, once he was sick with 23 miles left. He lost 500 guineas the first time, 2,000 the second. He trained hard and comfortably managed the same feat, and in front of thousands of spectators won 5,000 guineas. His stamina was phenomenal. One morning in August 1808 he went out at five o'clock to shoot grouse, covering 30 miles over the Grampians while he did so. He returned to Allanmore House where he ate dinner, and overnight walked to his house at Ury, near Stonehaven. That afternoon he walked sixteen miles to Lawrencekirk, danced at a ball and walked home, where he spent the day shooting partridge. Finally, after three days, he went to bed. The following June he walked 1,000 miles, one mile in each of 1,000 consecutive hours, snatching fragments of sleep when he could, and won 1,000 guineas. With one of his tenants he strode the length of the Highlands buying cattle.

This was one end of the scale, walking in the grand manner. At a simpler level was the traditional race at Carnwath, near Lanark, for the prize of a pair of red hose given by the landlord. Foot racing was universal at local games, but at the highest level gambling continued to be common. At the first meeting at the famous track at Powderhall on the north side of Edinburgh in 1869, dissatisfied backers chased the judge.

At this point athletics suddenly took on a large role in the public schools and universities all over Britain. The slogan was 'a healthy mind in a healthy body'. One result was the setting up of the Scottish Amateur Athletic Association in 1883, to provide competition that was free of bookmakers and professionalism. The first president was a schoolmaster.

In 1830 an English traveller visiting Montrose wrote

> The old Scots game of golf is a gigantic variety of billiards; the table being a certain space in the green, sometimes of many hundreds of yards in extent - the holes situated here and there at great distances; and the balls, which are very hard, stuffed with feathers, being swung to and fro by means of long queues with elastic shafts, - a fine healthful game.

A fine healthful game, indeed, if not completely understood. Golf at the beginning of the century was almost confined to the links on the east coast where it had been played for centuries. The spread began around the time of the invention of the 'gutty', the solid ball made of gutta percha which replaced the 'feathery'

Caddies, golfers, spectators and weather on the west coast of Scotland, 1892. SEA

which the Englishman had seen. The gutty was cheaper and could be driven further, and it had the useful property, especially in putting, of retaining its shape. Golf became easier, courses longer. Soon it was taken up elsewhere. English holidaymakers made for Scotland, and *Punch* published a cartoon of them massed on the fairways, labelled 'The Golf Stream'. The Open Championship was first held in 1860: it was won by a Scot every year until 1888, by a Briton until 1907 and by a European until 1921. By this time the game had again been reshaped by a new ball, the American rubber-core ball. Scotland still has more golf courses in relation to the size of its population than any other country in the world, and whilst in other places the game is almost entirely in the hands of private clubs, Scotland has many public courses.

In Scotland quoiting, usually pronounced 'kiting', was a sport in which heavy metal rings, usually weighing 8 to 12 lbs (3.6 to 5.5 kg), but sometimes as heavy as 23 lb (10.5 kg), were thrown at a pin in the ground. The distance of the throw varied: 22 yards was a common length. Quoiting was in its essentials the same game as curling or bowls, but could be played on rough ground. There is some evidence that it was originally played by the gentry, but by the nineteenth century it was a working man's sport, 'this ancient, manly and friendly game'. It grew rapidly in the middle of the century, replacing hainching. At a competition in Ayrshire in 1834 it was said that the losing finalists had for six hours been throwing quoits, 'a couple of which would almost be a load for a Glasgow porter'. The same report added: 'We should like to see our gentry taking an interest in this sport. The game has nothing of the brutality of the English prize-ring, while it possesses all that is necessary to prevent the people from sinking into that state of enervation and effeminacy which is the certain precursor of the decline and fall of all empires.' The gentry did not take up the sport: quoiting was for many years associated with gambling and heavy drinking. Many quoiting rinks were beside pubs; quoiting was not quite respectable. It was a betting sport and it is no surprise to find that in a dispute after a match at Milton of Balgonie

The Cathcart family at a cricket match at Schawpark, Alloa, painted by David Allan in 1785. The boy is holding a caman: *shinty was still common in the lowlands in the eighteenth century.*

The King as master of the hunt, about 1510. James IV with a peregrine falcon, detail from a painting by Daniel Mytens (died 1656), based on an earlier portrait.

Left

Horse racing on the sands at Leith, 1859. Detail from a painting by Alexander Reed. This was the last year of a great popular festival.

A shooting party in the Highlands, detail from a painting by Richard Ansdell (1815–85), 1840.

Above

Curling at Duddingston by Charles Altamont Doyle.

'Now strike!' - 'No! draw:' -
    'Come, fill the port,'
They roar, and cry, and blether;
As round the tee we flock wi' glee,
In cauld, cauld, frosty weather.

One of the pair of toddy bowls given to Delvine Curling Club by their President in 1832.

Frequent, meanwhile, the curlers' roar
Rolls round the meadow's icy shore.

Gold teapot, the King's Prize at Leith, won by 'Legacy', 1737, made by James Ker, Edinburgh, when tea was a costly drink for the gentry.

'Flying tackle' by Hamish Campbell. In the 1990s rugby is at a turning point with the sport generating increasingly large sums of money, at the same time as demanding huge commitment from unpaid players.

Rosebery football sweater worn by Walter White when he played against England in 1907. Scotland sometimes used Lord Rosebery's racing colours, which were derived from his title and family name, Primrose - primrose and rose.

*Heavy horse race at the Royal
Highland Show, Ingliston, 1989.*
Douglas Low

*The cover of the Border League
rugby fixture card for 1932-3.*

'Winning by a street' by Hamish Campbell. Sport is for everyone, and sports for the disabled have developed greatly in the last quarter-century.

New ways of enjoying the country-side: hang-gliding and paragliding became popular in the 1970s.
Harry Morgan

The Athens marathon, 1993. The two Scots have given their Kilmarnock bonnets to South African runners. This race has particular significance because of the Greek origin of the marathon.

Country sports in the city: boys fishing in the Clyde at Dalmarnock, 1991. John Burnett

in Fife 'fists and quoits were thrown'. At nearby Leslie the sport
was banned by the Town Council in 1858.

Quoiting declined from the First World War almost to extinction in the mid 1960s. Strength was essential, and the sport
shrank along with Scotland's heavy industry, and with the rapid
fall in the number of farm labourers. It still, however, survives on
a small scale in half a dozen scattered towns, from Canonbie to
Stonehaven.

8 Curling and bowling

Under the heading 'Curliana' the *Ayr Advertiser* announced in
February 1823:

> The following and many other communications on this subject
> have been sent to us by our persevering Correspondents. If they be
> of little interest to the world in general, they appear of much con-
> sequence to the parties concerned.

The parties were numerous: curling was by far the most common
sport in Scotland in the nineteenth century. Only the rise of football as a spectator sport at the end of the century challenged it,
and football was partly a product of the growth of the cities.
Curlers expressed their great enthusiasm for their sport in many
ways: by playing all day and into the moonlit night, by awarding
more medals than any other sport, by convivial dinners of 'beef
and greens'. More than any other Scottish game, curling produced a host of songs which were sung at these dinners. Many of
the songs celebrated nothing more - or nothing less - than a
wholehearted enjoyment of the game and the socializing afterwards. There was little relationship between teetotalism and
curling.

Curling was already popular when John Cairnie (about 1769-
1842) took to the ice. He was a retired surgeon whose professional
life had been spent in India, and he made his home in Largs with
the intention of enjoying sailing and bowling in summer, and

curling in winter. As a full-time sportsman he was frustrated by mild weather melting the ice on the ponds, so he invented the artificial pond, shallow and clay-lined. He found he had quadrupled the number of days on which he could curl.

Cairnie was the first chairman of the Grand Caledonian Curling Club, founded in 1838 and 'Royal' from 1842. It was Scotland's first national sporting society, its aim to encourage competition between clubs, and the pages of its *Annual* and the many RCCC surviving medals show its success.

There were many curling tales. The curlers of Wanlockhead had the advantage that the altitude of their village, high up in the Lowther Hills, made the ice last longer and gave them more time to perfect their skills. When the men of Sanquhar, the next parish to the west, were boasting that they could beat anyone on earth and would have to go to the Moon to find anyone to give them a match, someone said, 'Aye, but tell them to ca' at Wanlockhead on the way up.' It was in Sanquhar, too, that after a heavy defeat individual skips' scores were chalked on their doorposts, and the full margin of defeat on the Town Hall door. There could not be a better illustration of sport involving the whole community.

Bowling is an ancient game which exists in several forms. Long bowls and hainching or road bowling take place over large dis-

Inkstand in the form of a curling stone, Penicuik Curling Club, 1838.

tances, and were popular before the nineteenth century, though quite dangerous. Lawn bowls was for the few who could afford a smooth green. There were a few greens in burghs, and some country houses had one. Towards the end of the eighteenth century there were two in Glasgow and at least three in Edinburgh: the silver trophy of the Edinburgh Society of Bowlers suggests the kind of person who was likely to win it: a merchant or professional man.

In 1814 an 11-year-old boy named William Mitchell joined the bowling club at Kilmarnock - founded in 1740 and the oldest club in existence today. Mitchell became a solicitor and with his legal expertise drafted the first Laws of Bowling in 1849. His *Manual of Bowl Playing* (1861) was the first textbook on the sport. He was said to be 'the Nestor and Solon of bowls', a wise man indeed. Bowls grew because men had greater leisure, and it appealed to older men. In the First World War clubs lamented the deaths of a few members but of far more members' sons. The nature of the play was similar to curling, but it did not need the strength which was needed for quoiting. The other stimulus was the Earl of Eglinton. The Eglinton Cup for competition between the clubs of Glasgow and those of Ayrshire started in 1857, and he visited matches, played at many clubs and promoted the sport.

The Scots gave bowling four elements of its worldwide success. First, as a contemporary put it, they took the game from the 'low surroundings' of public houses, and made it respectable. Despite this, many clubs have floated on profits from their bars. Second, Mitchell's laws and their descendant the Scottish Bowling Association's laws of 1893, are the basis of the laws used all over the world. Third, the Scots showed the advantage of using the highest quality of turf on greens, so that skill was emphasized and the element of luck reduced. The most important source of turf during the mid-Victorian growth of bowls was the links by the Clyde - and here again we have to notice that the Earl of Eglinton supplied half a dozen greens from his land on the coast around Irvine. Fourthly, the Scots were the first to provide municipal greens.

Edinburgh Corporation Bowling Tournament on the public greens at Balgreen, about 1955.

Some bowling clubs were a part of the social life of members' families. At Shawlands in 1872

> Saturday last was a gala day in this rising suburb, the occasion being the opening of the eleventh season of the bowling club. The president provided an excellent quadrille band and piano. Dancing commenced on the greensward adjoining the bowling green ... a plentiful supply of cake and wine was provided ...

This was bowling for the middle classes. The growth of bowls as a sport for the working man took place slowly between 1850 and 1950. In 1850 there were about 30 clubs, and by 1882 there were 400 with 30,000 members, and now there are 1,000 clubs in Scotland.

To see bowling as a part of Scotland, visit the small Burgh of Wigtown. The High Street opens from street-width at the west end to be a hundred yards wide at the east, with two-storied

W W Mitchell (died 1884),
Kilmarnock solicitor and author
of the first laws of bowling.

Archibald William Montgomerie,
13th Earl of Eglinton (1812-61),
one of the great patrons of sport in
Victorian Scotland.

buildings, homes and shops, down the two sides. The plan is medieval, and until the eighteenth century cattle were driven in from the fields every evening, to spend the night in the High Street. The east end is closed by the mid-Victorian County Buildings. In front of them, in the middle of the High Street, is the bowling green. It is surrounded by the burgh's life.

9 Patronage and competition

We have already seen the Earl of Eglinton's enthusiasm for sport stemming from his wish to re-create the Middle Ages. The way in which he tried to do this was to make himself patron of many sports. The idea occurred to him at the great Tournament of 1839 which

> inaugurated, if it did not indeed suggest, LORD EGLINTON's life-long confidence in the masses; and his long cherished opinions, that if the state or the aristocracy wish to elevate the working-classes, out-door amusements, recreations in public parks, &c., free mingling of classes in innocent pastime, will do more to raise the self-respect of the humble, and to fortify them against intemperance and vicious courses, than the most eloquent sermons or the severest statutes.

The meeting of the Irvine Toxophilites in 1846 illustrates the ritual and pageantry which Eglinton encouraged: he would have been satisfied with his obituary which referred to 'the archery meetings so suggestive of the merry greensward of long-gone summers'. Dressed in club uniforms, the archers assembled at the Eglinton Arms. The Glasgow club wore dark green, 'profusely braided on the breast'; the Partick, light green with gold facings; and the Irvine Toxophilites themselves were also dressed in light green. The Earl wore a dark green frock with matching facings (the medieval imitation is clear), a broad belt with a silver clasp and long white gloves, plus the president's white silk sash and a feather in his bonnet.

Eglinton encouraged a wide range of sports by giving prizes for them. There was the Eglinton Collar for hare coursing, and the Eglinton Stakes for bitch puppies. At bowls the Eglinton Cup

The trophies of an ordinary sportsman, Peter Bourhill (1884-1948) of Newtongrange, including a clock for coming third in the three mile walk at Glasgow Rangers' sports (1903), and a cricket ball for scoring a century (1929).

was for competition between the clubs of Ayrshire and clubs of Glasgow, and a gold medal for clubs connected with the Eglinton estates. The Eglinton Tankard was for cricket. Prestwick and Prestwick Mechanics' Golf Clubs received medals: a gold medal for the gentry and professional men, a silver for the Mechanics'. Perhaps his most famous piece of silverware was the Eglinton Cup for curling rinks in Ayrshire, first played for in 1851 and still the leading trophy in Ayrshire. Among many others were prizes for shooting for the Volunteers, who had a large camp and ranges at Ardrossan. He also presented the championship belt for the Open Golf championship (1860). The 14th Earl followed his father by presenting prizes for competition in Ayrshire, such as a silver quoit (1862), and a gold cup for cricket (1868).

We should pause here and notice a subtle shift. The winners of traditional competitions such as the Kilwinning arrow or the Edinburgh Bowling Club's silver jack did not gain a trophy. They won the right to add a medal to it: the archer or the bowler gave something to posterity. Victorian prizes were to be kept, and the action of giving was replaced by the lesser act of taking.

What was the result of these prizes? Winning became important to the players. When John Lyon, the local baker, presented a pair of bowls to Galston Bowling Club in 1862 they 'tended to cause a spirit of emulation among the members'. The winner was not only someone who had been successful on one afternoon - he was the possessor of a symbol of his superiority for a year, and through his name engraved on the trophy, for life. John Lyon's prize was one which would be seen every time the bowls were used in a match: they were a message to the bowlers. A silver plate on the dresser or a cup on the sideboard were to be seen by everyone who entered the room.

At the Kirkcaldy regatta in 1872 the prizes were presented by a worthy and wordy bailie. At the end of his speech a yachtsman added that if he had himself been as successful in the race of life as he had been on the water, he would have been a bailie too. No doubt there was laughter, but the truth beneath was that life was becoming more competitive, and sport was a part of life and an image of it.

Michaelson Porteous (1796-1872) of Maybole wrote a lament on the death of a bowler, in imitation of Burns:

> O' skips the vera pink was he,
> At countin' shots aye dour to see
> A' bools but his ain side's aglee,   squint
>   Whilk he'd maintain:
> Though I'se no vrite that he would lee,
>   Auld Jamie gane.

The spirit is quite different from Burns, or any eighteenth-century bowler. Auld Jamie may be enjoying his sport, but he is determined to win.

10 Professional and spectators

The earliest professional sportsmen were the hunters and game-keepers, and the bowyers and fletchers who made the bows and arrows for the aristocrats and the men who hunted and practised archery. Their number was small. By the late seventeenth century there were still only a few who made their living from sport, but the work they did was varied.

Sir John Foulis's account books show the way that men might make part of their living from sport. There were the makers of the golf clubs and balls which he bought. There was also Pratt, on whose bowling green Sir John played in 1703-6: an entrepreneur who laid out a venue, and then took a profit from it. We have already come across Tamson's green. Another was Tom Bicket's at Kilmarnock. Later came Sparkes' cricket ground at Edinburgh. In England the name of a promoter of this kind lives on at Lord's. When Sir John went coursing the 'hare finder' was paid - probably a farm hand who received little other than bed and board. When he golfed he gave four shillings to 'the boy yt carried my clubs when my lord Regr (the Lord Clerk Register) and newbyth was at the links'(1672). Most likely the boy was a servant of one of his friends. When Sir John bought a football, it must have been from a saddler, who was one of many who made a little money from sport.

The professional played a large part in introducing new sports to Scotland, particularly by teaching. John Sparkes, cricketer, came from London to the Grange club in Edinburgh in 1833 or 1834. He was employed to show the members how to play. He was nearly 60 years old when he arrived, but most of his successors were young Yorkshiremen who hoped to go to a better paid job in England. A few did so: Wilfred Rhodes, who between 1899 and 1930 took more wickets than anyone else in the history of first-class cricket, was professional at Galashiels in 1896-7. These young men were expected to win matches for their club as well as to coach. Percival King from Surrey was the complete professional: player, teacher, arranger of big matches, owner of a sports shop in Edinburgh, and publisher of *Percival King's Scottish Cricketers' Annual and Guide*.

The way in which one man might play several roles can be seen in the development of the golf professional. At the beginning of the nineteenth century there were caddies carrying clubs, professionals who played with the amateurs and were paid for their advice, and club and ball makers. As the game became more

A group of feathery golf balls, about 1840. Each one is filled with as many feathers as would fill a top hat.

*'The Golfers' (1847) by Charles Lees (1800-80). The match
was a foursome between leading amateurs played in 1844.
The great professional and golf ball maker, Allan Robertson,
is on the left.*

popular and the number and quality of courses increased, new
specialisms emerged. Allan Robertson (1815-59) of St Andrews,
who made balls marked ALLAN because there were others of his
family in the same business, was the first man who could make a
living from his skill as a player, by winning matches for money.
Tom Morris, a pupil of Robertson, was the first great 'keeper of
the green', superintending the course and the players at
Prestwick from 1851 and at St Andrews from 1863; he also
designed courses. He was a fine player who won the Open

Championship for the fourth time in 1867, and his exceptional son won it in 1868-70.

Fox-hunting depended on the skills of huntsmen, many of whom were English. They could have a career by moving from hunt to hunt, perhaps starting as a second whip and ending with the most senior job, huntsman. John Squires was such a man. He joined the Lanarkshire and Renfrewshire Hunt in 1862. He had been born in Hampshire and died after a fall from a horse near Bridge of Weir. The operation of the hunt depended on him, and on the earthstopper, the kennelman, and the other hunt servants.

The growth of professional sport, however, centres on football. Football in Scotland grew rapidly after the formation of the Queen's Park club in 1867. England developed the game more quickly and there was a demand for quality players: well before the payment of players was officially allowed, footballers were

Hampden Park, home of Queen's Park FC and the Scottish team's usual home venue. There have been three Hampden Parks, and this is the third, opened in 1903. SEA

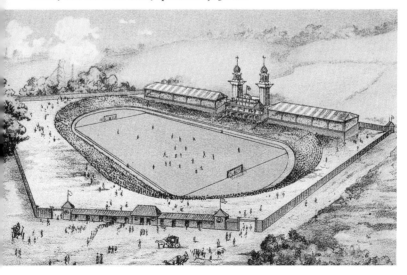

receiving money, and the clubs in the north of England had a particular eye for Scotsmen. Professionalism was introduced in England in 1885, in Scotland in 1893. The new element was the spectator, the sporting enthusiast who did not play but was willing to pay week after week to watch others. Crowds paying gate-money were able to fund the players' wages, and usually leave a profit for the club whose owners were often in the drink trade. It was a time when the spending power of ordinary people was rising. Football was one result. Others were days at the seaside at Portobello or on a Clyde steamer, or nights at the music hall where the comedian on the stage would tell jokes about the comedians on the local football park.

11 Victorian field sports

We have already seen royalty in the hunting field. The long history of the chase is closely linked to the owners of land. Around 1840 what had been an activity for Highland lairds only extended to a wider world which involved more people, all of them monied, whatever their origin.

The most distinctively Victorian of field sports was deer-stalking - distinctive because it was not common until Prince Albert took it up. Fashion followed royalty, and soon staghounds were a thing of the past and 'shooting boxes' appeared in the bleakest and most remote areas. Corrour Old Lodge was built above Rannoch Moor at a height of 1,723 feet (525 m), said to have been the highest house in Britain. The number of deer killed was recorded, their weight, their quality: this was industry in the glens. It was an aristocratic sport, dominated by English visitors, though it is impossible to ignore the eccentric American millionaire Walter Winans. By the 1880s he had acquired shooting rights over a vast tract of land from the Great Glen to the west coast. He had contempt for stalking: to him, shooting a deer was too easy if the animal was standing still. His passion was for deer driving, shooting running deer. He would do it almost every day for the six weeks of the season. His energy was extraordinary. He believed that every man should learn to shoot, since this was the only way to ensure the survival of the nation, a strange echo of the medieval requirement to practise archery on Sunday, hinting also at trench warfare in Flanders thirty years later.

Pheasant and grouse shooting expanded after about 1840, and attracted many wealthy Englishmen and women to the Scottish moors, especially after the Queen had fallen in love with the Highlands. It remained popular until the Second World War: the first time the British Cabinet met outside London was in September 1921, at Inverness. The most determined sportsmen organized shooting as a production line with division of labour among the participants. A highly skilled shot might have four double-barrelled shotguns and two men to load them, and the maximum size of bag was sought. Game books proudly recorded not only game birds, but crows, magpies and domestic cats that had escaped. One writer praised the difficulty of finding and shooting blackgame - blackcock and greyhen - 'should a brace be secured single-handed one feels much prouder of the achievement than if one had assisted to fill a game cart full of pheasants'.

The hammer in the ironworks never moved more rapidly than the hammers on the shotguns.

Far more people were stalking deer and shooting birds, but one field sport almost vanished. This was falconry, which had many pre-industrial aspects: it was really a craft. The training of a

Sir John Gilmour and Mrs Hardcastle shooting in Ross-shire, 1906. SEA

Sir John Maxwell of Pollok (1768-1844), mezzotint by
Charles Turner (1816), after a painting by James Howe.
Maxwell was one of the enthusiasts behind the rapid growth
of fox-hunting in Scotland.

falcon took months if not years, and the bird had to be trained by
the falconer who was going to fly it. This did not appeal to the
casual arrival at a shooting lodge just in time for the Glorious
Twelfth of August. At the most only a couple of dozen kills could
be made in a day. It was a manipulation of nature rather than an
assault, and it gave an aesthetic pleasure. In August 'no more
beautiful sight can be witnessed than that of a high-coupled
Falcon 'stopping' downward from an immense height and
hurling it headlong into the heather.' The line of professional falconers died out with Peter Ballantyne of Ochiltree about 1870.
The survival of the sport depended on a few amateurs.

Fox-hunting for sport behind a pack of hounds began in
England in the late seventeenth century, during the period after

the restoration of the monarchy when sport was fashionable. At first it grew slowly: the oldest Scottish hunts still in existence are probably the Berwickshire and the Liddesdale, both in the field by 1740. At the end of the eighteenth century foxes were so troublesome to sheep that some parishes gave head-money to anyone who killed one, and others paid a salary to a full-time hunter. Fox-hunting spread, reaching its peak before the First World War. The number of Scottish hunts has since fallen, and six of the ten now in existence are in the Borders.

12 Games in the Highlands and Highland games

Deer-stalking and other forms of hunting in the Highlands have been described above as sport for visitors, but for the Highland people they had since time immemorial been on the border between sport and the need to eat. The successful hunter was a hero. The Gaelic poet Duncan Bàn McIntyre (1724-1803), a member of the Edinburgh town guard, addressed the captain of the guard, Duncan Campbell:

> In all manly sports thou wast adept
> for the ranging of rough mountain regions;
> thou wast the best of hunters
> to go forth and slay the hind;
> in the glades of the woodland
> or in the twig-tangled thicket,
> thou wast death to the woodcock
> that crew early in the May morning.

Both Macintyre and Campbell came from Argyllshire.

Shinty is the distinctive Highland sport. It is a very old game. It was certainly played more than 2,000 years ago, and it is mentioned often, both in Scotland and Ireland, in early Celtic literature. Cuchullin, that hero of heroes, when a boy went to Emin Macha, on the east coast of Ireland, and single-handed won a game against 150 boys. He played with a brass *caman* (stick) and a silver ball. Later, his uncle sent him to Skye to improve his game.

Down to the early nineteenth century shinty was highly popular in the Gàidhealtachd, but it was also played in Lowland Scotland and parts of England. The children in the cotton mills at New Lanark, founded in 1784, played shinty. Games in which the whole male population of a parish joined were common in the Highlands and Islands at New Year, and it was commonly played by boys going to and from church. The wave of puritanism which passed over the Highlands in the middle of the century curtailed sport on Sundays and other pastimes limited the time free for shinty. In 1793 the minister of Moulin in Perthshire wrote:

> It is observable that gymnastic exercises, which constituted the chief pastimes of the Highlands forty or fifty years ago, have almost entirely disappeared. At every fair or meeting of the country people there were contests of racing, wrestling, putting the stone, etc.; and on holidays all the males of the district, young and old, met to play at football, but oftener at shinty. These games are now practised only by schoolboys, having given place to the more elegant but less manly amusement of dancing.

Shinty reached its lowest ebb in the middle of the nineteenth century. It was wiped out in the Lowlands because the police stopped it being played in its usual venue, the streets, thinking it was dangerous.

The rules and equipment of shinty were different in different places. A two-handed caman was widely used, but the one-handed version was preferred in Kintyre and in adjacent Antrim. In some places the ball was thrown up in the air to start play, in others such as Lewis it was lightly buried and players had to unearth it with their sticks. In Argyllshire the ball was wooden, in Badenoch a leather skin tightly stuffed with hair.

In 1880 Captain Archibald Chisholm of Glassburn wrote the first standard rules for shinty. He was determined that the game should not die and realized that as transport was becoming better, it was easier for men from different districts to arrange fixtures. A match at Inverness in 1887 between Strathglass and Glenurquhart attracted interest and more than 30 clubs had been formed by the winter of 1892/3. In 1893 the Camanachd Association was set up. In Ireland, the Gaelic Athletic Association had been founded in 1884 to promote sports which were seen as being non-English such as handball, Gaelic football and shinty's sibling, hurling. It was closely linked to political nationalism. The revival of shinty can be seen as part of a pan-European enthusiasm for national identity which was expressed in the music of Sibelius and Smetana, and the politics of Garibaldi. International hybrid shinty-hurling matches have been played since 1972.

Scottish shinty players versus Irish hurlers by Jim Galloway (1988). Note the difference between the slender-ended caman *and the broad Irish hurley on which the ball can be carried.*

Highland Games, despite the artificial pageantry attached to some of the more famous games, are based on sports that have traditions as deep as the piping and dancing which take place alongside them. The first 'modern' games were held in St Fillans in Perthshire in 1819. The Braemar Gathering has its origin in a Friendly Society which, like the carters with their horse racing, started an annual games. Its character changed when Queen Victoria arrived in 1848.

Many say that the most atmospheric games are those at Glenfinnan, held on the Saturday nearest 19th August, the anniversary of the landing of Prince Charles Edward Stuart in 1745. The first

Putting the stone from McIan's The Highlanders at Home *(1848). Highland gatherings were to some extent a nineteenth-century invention, but some of the sports, like this one, were ancient.*

meeting, in 1845, began with a commemorative speech, then 'the ladies and gentlemen present joined the peasantry', as though the gentry only were allowed access to certain parts of Scottish history. Then began 'the usual national and characteristic games'. There is an uncomfortable feeling that the Highland people were themselves part of the spectacle.

The 'light' events were running and jumping, as practised all over the country. The 'heavy' events were putting the shot, throwing the hammer and tossing the caber. From the mid-1850s to around 1880 the leading figure was Donald Dinnie (1837-1916) of Aboyne. He was a stonemason and performed feats of dressing granite and building walls, working against time for wagers. One of his most famous throws with the hammer went into the crowd and hit a cameraman from a London athletics magazine who had been to photograph him. Dinnie's chief rival around 1870 was James Fleming:

> An' grand it was to ane an' a'
> To see him poise the iron ba',
> Then send it wi' a spring awa'
>   As clean's a quoit -
> While owre the lave an ell or twa   a measure of just over a yard
>   He garr'd it skyte!   made it fly

Dinnie and Fleming found there was good money to be made at games in America and Australia, and they travelled together. Later, A A Cameron (1875-1951) was a regular champion. Unlike Dinnie and Fleming he preferred farming to full-time professional athletics, and claimed that scything was the best form of exercise. Cameron came from Lochaber, and is one of the few sportsmen to have been commemorated in music, in *A A Cameron's Strathspey*.

The modern triple jump, or hop, step and jump, was also common in Victorian Scotland and was held at most Highland games. There were many variants: eight hops and a jump, or the hop, ten steps, and jump. This produced more events for betting.

It also showed the differences between one games and another, the existence or creation of local traditions, the opposite tendency to the standardization of rules which modern sport encourages.

13 Sports for all

The oldest sporting venues in Scotland are the traditional places of recreation such as the North Inch in Perth, the Boroughmuir in Edinburgh, and Glasgow Green. The space belonged to the people, but if they needed facilities for a particular sport, say a specially marked out area, they had to arrange it themselves.

The burghs began to provide sporting facilities towards the end of the nineteenth century. The idea of the 'town's plate' for horse racing, or of prizes for bowling burgesses, had more or less died out at the beginning of the Victorian era: most of these prizes had been for a social élite. Before 1900, town councils found ways of helping ordinary people to enjoy their recreation. First were many more public parks. Land was found in dozens of towns, gardens laid out, benches put in place, fountains and bandstands built. Walter Macfarlane of Glasgow, who cast the curliest ironwork, made large profits. Philanthropy was common as landlords gave land and sometimes paid for sporting facilities: one of the first was Sir Michael Shaw Stewart who in 1852 provided a quoiting ground, bowling green and cricket pitch in addition to Well Park itself, for the people of Greenock. Several towns had ponds for model boats. Later came football pitches, golf courses and tennis courts. The first indoor swimming pools were as much for giving baths to tenement dwellers as for sport, but sport was always there. An early example is Greenhead Baths in Glasgow, opened in 1878, with its 'swimming pond'.

Companies also laid out sports grounds for their employees. Sport was seen as being healthy, and encouraged loyalty to the firm and the team spirit. In Edinburgh, the Caledonian Brewery's bowling green can be seen beside Slateford Road, and the much more recent IBM factory near Greenock has a green too. The

North British Rubber Company, the biggest employer in Edinburgh, provided a range of sports facilities including a club for boys in the factory. In 1919 the Works Manager explained 'that the Club was intended to give the boys some other interest than their work, with the expectation and the hope that it would be beneficial both to the boys and their work'.

The clearest sign of the growing importance of sport in Scottish life was the popularity of football. Crowds were swelling before the First World War, and they grew again when the release from war brought a new enthusiasm for leisure. The Glasgow and Edinburgh teams drew big crowds, but even more people went to the matches against England, especially after the famous victory of the 'Wembley Wizards' in 1928. In 1931 129,000 were at Hampden Park, then a world record for a sporting event. Through the Depression of the 1930s football and the thought of football filled the time of the unemployed. Star Park at Newtongrange, on the edge of the Midlothian coalfield, was built with a capacity of 30,000 although it was only the home of a junior team.

In the fake prosperity caused by preparation for another war, crowds rose again: there were now enough wages to pay the gate money. The figures are staggering: the game against England in 1937 was watched by 149,415 people, and a week later the Scottish Cup Final drew 147,365. These are both records for crowds in Europe, for an international, and for a club game.

The great crowds survived into the 1960s. They grew smaller for a number of reasons: the growth of sports other than football, the movement of people away from the heart of the city to New Towns some distance from the grounds, and most of all the sudden spread of television. There was also a greater understanding of the fact that a huge uncontrolled crowd is a danger to the people in it. This was shown with terrible clarity at the end of the Rangers-Celtic match on 2 January 1971. The crowd began to leave before the final whistle, streaming down the stairs at the back of the terracing. Rangers scored a last-minute goal and in

*Football had covered the whole country by 1900. These are
Inverness Caledonian supporters nearly a hundred years
later. 'Scottish Cup Highlander's Delight' by Ken
McPherson.*

the excitement someone on Stairway 13 lost their footing. In the
crush no one could react: they could only fall and die, suffocated
under the weight of those behind them. Sixty-six people were
killed.

The footballer, with the help of newspapers, radio and latterly
television, became a hero. He was 'the King of Scotland', and in the
days when politicians were admired 'the Wee Prime Minister'.
Hibernian had the 'Famous Five'. Adulation and alcohol often
turned the hero's feet to clay, and many were forgotten in a year.
One Scot stands out from all the others, despite having been a good
player rather than a great one. Jock Stein (1922-85) managed
Glasgow Celtic from 1965 to 1978. They won the Scottish League

for nine consecutive years and in 1967 became the first British club to win the European Cup. This is probably the greatest achievement by a Scottish team in any sport, and it was due to Stein's knowledge and leadership. He motivated the players and inspired the spectators: 'A game without a crowd is nothing,' he said.

Celtic are the Catholic football team in Glasgow, Rangers the Protestant: religion has always coloured the relationship between the two members of 'The Auld Firm'. Football has been used to stress divisions between people. Football can also unite. Aberdeen has only one senior team, and when they were highly successful in the early 1980s, 'it was a great time to be in town ... everybody was together, talking about it, we all wanted the same thing ... we were proud to be Aberdonians'. In the European Cup Winners' Cup, which Aberdeen won in 1983, their strongest opponents were Bayern Munich. With a few minutes to play the score was 2-2 and Aberdeen had a free kick. Two players ran towards the ball and 'accidentally' collided, distracting the German defenders, and Aberdeen scored. It was a moment to savour, and Aberdonians did. For years.

Many sports became more commercial after the First World War. There were fewer people with leisure and wealth: large payments from a few were replaced by moderate payments by many. The Glasgow and South Western Railway advertised golf by issuing in 1922 a booklet on the 80 courses on its network. It was remorselessly enthusiastic. At Barassie 'in addition to ordinary bunkers there are fine clumps of rushes and whins'. The booklet showed how easy it was to reach the courses: at Bogside (Irvine) it was possible to stand on the first tee 50 minutes after leaving Glasgow. At Troon the Club had an entrance fee of fifteen guineas and the professional was the well-known Willie Fernie, but there were no less than three municipal courses: 'No introduction is necessary, and there is no Entrance Fee.' The modest course at Colvend, on the Galloway coast, was recommended because Fernie had laid it out.

Sports such as golf and tennis began to come within the reach of working people, as game shooting had expanded from the gentry to the professionals two generations earlier. Some local newspapers put forward political and social views through the medium of dialogues or discussions between imaginary characters who appeared week after week. Here is a contribution in the radical *Fifeshire Advertiser* of 1936:

> The workin' classes, when holiday time comes round, can aye manage to ape the better class, tho' they hae to be obleeged to the pawnbroker, for they think - an' quite richt they are - that they are entitled to the guid things o' the world, like sport an' pleasure, an' a share o' the bracin' air that's to be got on a gowf course.

The argument was over the opening of golf courses on Sunday. The *Advertiser* was strongly in favour since it was the only full day off work for most people.

In the same decades women's sport grew quickly. Middle-class women had golfed and played tennis before the First World War. The war showed that women had far more than a domestic role to play in society. Sporting clubs established women's sections and the patterns evolved on the model of sport for men.

Miss Pitcaithly of the Moncreiff Curling Club, Bridge of Earn, Perthshire, 1937.
SEA

Sports have extended themselves by moving out of their original environment, usually from outdoors to indoors. Indoor bowling was begun by the Edinburgh Winter Bowling Association in 1905, and there were still only a few indoor rinks fifty years later. Then came rapid expansion, and indoor and outdoor bowling are both very popular. In curling the situation was completely different. Until 1907 it was played on ponds, lochs and reservoirs. The opening of the first Crossmyloof Ice Rink in Glasgow depended on refrigerating machinery imported from across the Atlantic. In 1912 two indoor rinks opened in Edinburgh and one in Aberdeen. From 1927 the growth of ice hockey, which drew large crowds, encouraged the building of six more rinks before the war. The total today is over twenty and curling has become an all-year-round sport. However, it is less often played in the open air, and hundreds of curling ponds have fallen out of use.

Skiing was made more accessible by the building of the artificial slope at Hillend on the Pentlands. When it reached full size in 1965 it was the largest plastic slope in the world. The first all-weather athletics track in Scotland was opened at Grangemouth in 1966.

14 Scotland and the world

Britain has had the central role in the growth of sport and of international matches. Sport first became a mass enthusiasm here, and matches between Britain's four component nations were the forerunners of world sport. The first international matches at rugby and football took place in close succession in 1871 and 1872. Both were Scotland v England, and Ireland and Wales joined in later. The same pattern can be seen in other sports such as water polo and bowling. The first Scottish club to play football of any code in England was probably Glasgow Academicals who went to Lancashire for a rugby match in 1871. Queen's Park, Rangers and other football teams often played English teams in the last 30 years of the century.

Cricket, however, was the first sport in which teams from outside Britain - or Europe - played in Scotland. The Australians who toured England every three or four years from 1878 almost always came north. They excited great interest, not least among those who saw them binding together the British Empire.

Before the First World War sporting contact was made with Europe: Queen's Park went to Denmark in 1898. Raith Rovers also played played football there in 1922. A year later they went to the Canaries: the ship nearly sank, and they played a match in a bull ring, where one of the team tried to climb the boundary fence to attack abusive supporters. The national team first played football on the Continent in 1929 when in the space of ten days matches were played in Norway, Holland and Germany. Scotland did not meet a team from outside Europe until 1954, when they were beaten 7-0 by Uruguay in the World Cup in

Sporting tourists from the British Empire. The Australian cricket team of 1909 visiting a distillery.

Switzerland. Only after air travel was becoming common did they actually play outside Europe, first at Ankara in 1960. In the 1990s Glasgow Rangers would like to see themselves as a European team as much as a Scottish one.

There are four sports which Scotland has given to the world: golf, curling, bowling and rugby sevens.

Golf went south with James VI in 1603, and reached America several decades before the first club was formed in 1786. Its tremendous expansion in the USA took place, however, in the quarter of a century before the First World War. Charles Blair MacDonald, born in America but educated at St Andrews University, promoted the game, designed courses, ensured that the same rules were used, and was the winner of the first American Amateur Championship in 1895. The Royal Calcutta Golf Club was founded in 1829. Wherever there were Scots, there was golf, even if conditions were difficult. At Weihaiwei Island in China the suggested method for playing the short 9th was to bounce the ball off the clubhouse roof. A course over the volcanic ash on Ascension Island was completed in 1969.

Curling reached Canada at the same time as the Scots, and it went to the Alps when they became the 'sporting playground' for the wealthy. It was included in the first Winter Olympic Games, at Chamonix in 1924.

Bowling as a popular sport spread more slowly, first to England where for many years a leading figure was W G Grace, the great cricketer, who was a Licentiate of the Royal College of Physicians of Edinburgh. Grace was one of those behind the first series of international matches between Scotland, England, Ireland and Wales in 1903. Of the first seventeen series Scotland won twelve, its strength in this period showing its deeper experience and larger number of players. The World Bowls Board still issues its 'Laws of the Game (as originally formulated by the Scottish Bowling Association)'.

Rugby sevens, were invented in 1882 by Ned Haig, the Melrose butcher. Until after the First World War sevens tournaments were held only in the Borders. In the 1920s the Middlesex Sevens were started but the first international competition did not take place until 1973. The Border sevens, however, still have an intensity and a feeling of community which is unmatched at Twickenham, Hong Kong - or, indeed, Edinburgh.

Many sports, conversely, have come to Scotland from abroad. Pigeon-racing became a mass pursuit in Belgium in the middle of the nineteenth century. Greyhound racing, which is derived from hare coursing, originated in California. Speedway grew up in Australia and reached Britain in 1928. The Algonquin Indians, who were on the borders of the USA and Canada, played lacrosse, and it was adopted by Europeans in Canada who passed it across the Atlantic. Stockcar racing evolved in mountainous areas of America in the 1920s and 30s. It began as practice for escaping from the police seeking illegal liquor during the era of Prohibition. Judo and karate are from Japan. The Swedes invented orienteering and brought it to Scotland because they rightly believed that it had suitable and testing terrain. Pétanque, known in Britain as boules, is French.

Some sports for individual competitors operate on a British, European or world basis, and Scots have been successful in them. In golf, Sandy Lyle won the US Masters in 1988. Willie Carson, born in Stirling, has been Champion Jockey five times. In boxing Benny Lynch, a devastating puncher, was world flyweight champion in 1935-8. Jackie Patterson (1943-8) and Walter McGowan (1966) later held the same title and Ken Buchanan was world lightweight champion in 1970-2. Perhaps the most surprising achievement for a small country has been in Formula 1 motor racing. Jim Clark, a Berwickshire farmer, was world champion in 1963 and 1965, and Jackie Stewart in 1969, 1971 and 1973. Clark died in Belgium in a high-speed crash caused by a burst tyre, an accident which recalled the death of another Borderer, Jimmy Guthrie from Hawick. Guthrie had a successful career racing motor cycles, but was killed in 1937 on the last corner of the German Grand Prix. He was leading at the time.

15 Town and country

So far we have been looking at sports in which each event happens in one place. Other sports range over the countryside, such as walking, climbing, cycling, and skiing. Sometimes there is a competitive element, but often the aim is only the enjoyment of exercise in the open air.

John Taylor, a London waterman, set out one August for a walking tour of Scotland. He was a poet and eccentric who was forever borrowing money and would flatter anyone for a free dinner. He demands our attention, because the year was 1618, and he was the first English traveller to climb a Scottish mountain. He set out from Edzell 'where I found the valley very warm before I went up it; but when I came to the top of it, my teeth began to dance in my head with cold.' A familiar enough experience of Scottish weather. Taylor went

> Through heather, moors, 'mongst frogs, and bogs, and fogs,
> 'Mongst craggy cliffs, and thunder-battered hills

The path was rough and he was soaked by the time he reached Deeside, but he had climbed Mount Keen. Soldiers, hunters, drovers and men of business had been in the Scottish hills before Taylor: he was the first who has left a record of hill-walking in the hope of pleasure. Later tourists occasionally followed his example, most famously John Keats on Ben Nevis in 1818, and found it steep: 'it is almost like a fly crawling up a wainscote'.

Walking rapidly became popular in the nineteenth century as leisure increased and the railway network spread. It was particularly appealing to men and women who worked in mills, mines and foundries because it was an escape from darkness, discipline, dust and danger to the freedom of the moors and hills. Train services on Sundays were few: it was the Saturday half-holiday which opened up the open road - for there was little traffic. In 1885 Walter Smith's booklet *The Pentland Hills* appeared: the first guide purely for hill-walkers. Smith was involved with the

Scottish Rights of Way Society, who did sterling work in protecting rights of access to traditional paths. They also set up signs to guide walkers. At the same time, walking was appearing in literature. Robert Louis Stevenson's *Travels with a Donkey in the Cévennes* (1879) was not a book about France, but about a Scot walking through France. Stevenson compared the abrupt manners of the peasants with the behaviour of Fife people.

Walking at this period was usually done near the towns. The hills were for those with more time to spare. A common feature in the development of sports has been the discovery or invention of a sport by the wealthy, followed a generation or two later by its wider spread. Tennis is an example, and so are mountain sports. Towards the end of the nineteenth century professional and academic men started to go into the mountains in numbers, first to walk and then to climb. Sir Hugh Munro wrote his list of peaks

Climbers on a motorbike at Corran Ferry, 1935. Are they about to cross Loch Linnhe and make for the Ardgour hills, or return to Glasgow on the new road through Glencoe, opened three years before? SEA

over 3,000 feet high in 1890, offering a challenge. At the first dinner of the Scottish Mountaineering Club in 1889 the president damned those who went into the hills merely to gain another summit, 'not so much mountaineers as mountain acrobats'. The popularity of 'Munro bagging' now brings so many acrobats to the Highlands that they cause problems of erosion. Winter climbing, soon to become a particular feature in Scotland, was effectively begun at Easter 1894 when Norman Collie, a professor of chemistry, used Alpine techniques with ice axes in Glencoe and the Ben Nevis area. His activities in the Cuillin in Skye were commemorated by the naming of a mountain Sgùrr Thormaid, Norman's Peak. By the 1920s buses and lorries were leaving Glasgow at the weekends to take men and women to the hills, particularly the Arrochar Alps and Glencoe, in summer and winter. These people were mostly young and short of money - many were unemployed - and it was common to sleep rough, or in the open air. The *Daily Record*, the largest-selling daily newspaper, printed news and information about areas to visit. It provided propaganda for the Youth Hostel movement which had been started by German teacher, Richard Schirrman. Hostels gave spartan accommodation at a low price. The first in Scotland was opened in 1931 near Selkirk. Many were farm cottages, but there was also a disused church, a redundant brewery, and in Ayrshire the mansion of Dalquharran above the Water of Girvan. The German link was present for the first ten years. In 1936 the *Scottish Youth Hostel Handbook* included a page of welcome in German and listed a walking club in Glasgow called 'Die Deutsche sprechen Wanderer'. There was also an advertisement for holidays in Germany, taking in the Olympic Games in Berlin, the Games where Hitler tried to use sport to prove the superiority of the German people.

The same *Handbook* advised potential rock climbers:

Unless parties have had previous experience and are properly equipped for the job, or are accompanied by a guide of ripe experience, it is dangerous to venture on this fascinating pastime.

The conspicuous word in this sentence is 'fascinating': rock climbing became increasingly popular.

The hills provided escape, excitement and challenge. As the world lurched into Fascism, Communism and the shadow of war, the weekends gave a chance to talk over the shape of the world: left-wing politics were usual. At the same time, romance was in the air, and one climber recalled that his ideals came not from Marx but from Stevenson's *Songs of Travel:*

> Bed in the bush with stars to see,
> Bread I dip in the river –
> There's the life for a man like me,
> There's the life for ever.

In the 1880s walkers were joined by cyclists. An Englishman who toured the Highlands in 1881 was told by a ferryman that he was only the third 'wheelman' to reach Skye, and north of the Great Glen he attracted crowds of onlookers. He compared his own healthy travelling with tourists who sat in trains, missing all the best scenery because they were in a tunnel, whilst the cyclist was 'like the bee, free to settle where he pleases, and having taken the essence of out of one place, can flit to the next'. He encouraged others: 'let your object be to enjoy yourself, and to see the country intelligently.'

This man, who wrote under the pseudonym Nauticus, rode a tricycle on which he travelled 30 or 40 miles a day at, he said, eight or nine miles an hour on level ground. The state of the roads varied greatly, and from time to time Nauticus needed the help of blacksmiths to straighten out his machine. He was followed by many others, particularly after the development of the safety bicycle in the late 1880s, and the invention of the pneumatic tyre in 1888. As the price of bikes fell, more people could ride through the glens.

The story of skiing in Scotland begins with two men in the Campsies in 1892. Its growth has been continuous ever since. Before the First World War sports shops in Edinburgh received snow reports by electric telegraph and placed them in their

Cyclists at Bridge of Cally, Perthshire, about 1889. SEA

Nauticus on his cumbersome but robust tricycle, somewhere in the Highlands.

windows, and postmen were issued with skis in Deeside, Donside, Speyside and Sutherland. Although it originated in Norway, the Alps were the centre for the growth of skiing as a sport, and English skiers went there in large numbers in the 1920s. The collapse of the pound in 1932 brought them to Scotland, but the winter of 1932/3 was extraordinarily free of snow: in the first ten weeks more fell in Barcelona than Braemar, and Braemar was the centre on which the English had focused.

During the Second World War troops were trained in mountain warfare, including skiing, to create the possibility of invading Norway. Hitler was not fooled, but thousands of men discovered the sport. After the war ski tows and then chair lifts were installed, and as road transport became easier the numbers of sites and skiers increased. Commercial tows ennabled many more people

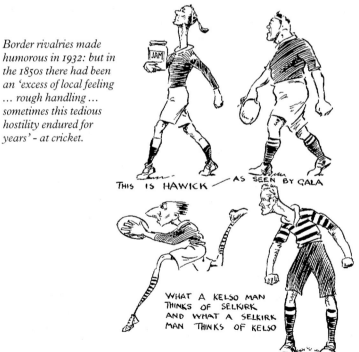

Border rivalries made humorous in 1932: but in the 1850s there had been an 'excess of local feeling … rough handling … sometimes this tedious hostility endured for years' - at cricket.

THIS IS HAWICK — AS SEEN BY GALA

WHAT A KELSO MAN THINKS OF SELKIRK AND WHAT A SELKIRK MAN THINKS OF KELSO

to reach the slopes in the late 1950s and early 1960s, particularly in Glencoe, Glenshee and the Cairngorms. Cheap flights opened the Alps and later the Rockies to the Scots: the airport departure lounge is now part of the sporting scene.

The best of Scotland's sporting literature writes of the mountains and moors. Sir Henry Alexander, in the unpromising format of a guidebook, described the plant, animal and human life of the Cairngorms with an understanding that has never been matched. In *Mountaineering in Scotland* (1946) WH Murray gave a series of essays on famous rock climbs in which he said much about the relationship between the climber and the climb. Most vividly of all Tom Patey's *One Man's Mountains* (1971) talks of mountaineers, incompetence, triumph, enthusiasm and failure in a book full of humanity, tragically published after Patey had fallen to his death whilst abseiling off a sea stack. Television changes some sports by making them international, and some would say they lose some of their character: walking in the Scottish countryside remains a purely Scottish experience.

16 Afterword

'Numerous disciples of Walton have been lashing the Leven with lines' wrote a Victorian journalist. This book has said nothing about angling, said to be the most popular sport in Britain. There has been no space for others: basketball, tenpin bowling, canoeing, race cycling, hockey, equestrianism, fencing, netball, polo, power boating, swimming, wrestling ... Many more might have been discussed at greater length, not least football.

Sporting events, like other emotional experiences, mark the months and the years. On a spring evening in 1988 the Border League decider was played between Jedforest and Kelso at the Greenyards in Melrose, where the outliers of the Lammermuirs rise at one end of the ground and the triple peaks of the Eildons at the other. The landscape enclosed the passionate rivalry between two Border towns, made sharper because Kelso had been the dominant team in Scotland for a couple of years, whereas Jed had a young side which was strengthening by the week. There was a sense of the passage of time: Kelso were ageing, and the great international career of Roy Laidlaw, Jed's scrum-half, had just ended. Kelso led, and the sun's and the season's long shadows fell across the field. In the last moments Laidlaw ran one way, stepped the other, made a gap in the defence: Jed won by a whisker. The shape of the season was decided in a few seconds. In a short but highly meaningful moment the previous eight months' rugby was put in its place.

The sharpness of the experience of sport lies in the significance of the instants when skill and the passage of action create the decisive opportunity. The depth of the experience lies in understanding all the influences, forces and past moments which interact to make the moment possible.

The Grand Curling match at Lochwinnoch in 1850 was one of the first games to be contested by a large number, when 'It's north o' the Clyde 'gainst the southern side'. There were over a thousand curlers on the ice:

See the rinks are a' marshalled, how cheerily they mingle,	
Blithe callants, stout chields, and auld grey-headed men,	striplings young men
Till their loud roaring stanes gar the snowy heights tingle	make
As they ne'er did before, and may never again.	

No one there could ever have forgotten the day, when

The ploughs o' the Lothians stand stiff i' the furrow,
And the weavers o' Beith for the Loch leave the loom.

And they did meet again, to abandon work and 'cheerily mingle' - Grand Matches are still held in the hardest winters - but every meeting is different, and the meeting of people makes up the history of sport.

PLACES TO VISIT

The British Golf Museum, St Andrews, is the only museum of the history of sport in Scotland which is open at present. Many local museums have sporting relics, often trophies and badges which have been colected as silver.

The Scottish Football Museum, based in Glasgow, does not have a permanent display, but arranges temporary exhibitions at various venues. The Scottish Rugby Union has a museum at Murrayfield; at the time of writing it is closed for reconstruction.

The oldest structure in Scotland built for sport is the tennis court at Falkland Palace (c.1540), but there has been far more sport on famous public spaces such as Glasgow Green, the North Inch at Perth, and Edinburgh's Boroughmuir. Golf was played on Leith Links five hundred years ago. At one end of the Links is an unusual survival, Seafield Baths of 1811-3, now a public house. Another oddity in Edinburgh is the curling house beside Duddingston Loch (1824): at the same date identical buildings were being erected beside burial grounds as watch towers against grave robbers.

Many of the most famous sporting venues - Ibrox, Celtic Park, Hampden, Murrayfield - have been rebuilt several times so that their historical character is obliterated. The stand at Inverleith rugby ground is a survival from the period up to 1925 when it was used for internationals. This is true of much more modest grounds, too. It can be interesting to look for fragments of sporting history where they occur.

Lastly, sport is primarily for playing. The Scottish Sports Council (Caledonian House, South Gyle, Edinburgh EH12) can provide information about clubs active in almost every sport in Scotland.

FURTHER READING

The best general reference book on sport is:

ARLOTT, John (ed.) *The Oxford Companion to Sport*, London 1975.

A good and well-illustrated summary of the rules of a wide range of sports can be found in:

THE DIAGRAM GROUP *The Rules of the Game*, London 1991.

On the history of sport in Scotland:

BUCHANAN, Margaret *Archery in Scotland: an Elegant and Manly Amusement* Glasgow 1979.

DONALD, Brian *The Fight Game in Scotland*, Edinburgh 1988.

FAIRFAX-BLAKEBOROUGH, James *History of Horse Racing in Scotland*, Whitby 1973. Northern Turf History, vol.4.

FITTIS, Robert Scott *Sports and Pastimes of Scotland*, Paisley 1891.

GEDDES, Olive *A Swing through Time: Golf in Scotland 1457-1743*, Edinburgh 1992.

HART-DAVIS, Duff *Monarchs of the Glen: the History of Deer-Stalking in the Scottish Highlands*, London 1978.

JARVIE, Grant *Highland Games: the Making of a Myth*, Edinburgh 1991.

JARVIE, Grant, and WALKER, Graham (eds) *Scottish Sport in the Making of the Nation*, London 1994.

KERR, John *History of Curling*, Edinburgh 1890.

MCCARRA, Kevin *Scottish Football: an Illustrated History from 1867 to the Present Day*, Glasgow 1984.

MCCONNELL, T *The Tartan Turf: Scottish Racing, its History and Heroes*, Edinburgh 1988.

MCGLONE, David, and MCLURE, Bill *The Juniors - 100 Years: a Centenary History of Scottish Junior Football*, Edinburgh 1987.

MACLENNAN, Hugh Dan *Shinty!*, Nairn 1993.

MAGNUSSON, Sally *The Flying Scotsman: a Biography*, London 1981. On the sprinter, rugby player and missionary, Eric Liddell.

'Bicycle Polo' by Ian Hossack.

MASSIE, Allan *A Portrait of Scottish Rugby*, Edinburgh 1984.

MURRAY, Bill *The Old Firm: Sectarianism, Sports and Society in Scotland*, Edinburgh 1984.

MURRAY, W H *The Curling Companion*, Glasgow 1981.

ORR, Willie *Deer Forests, Landlords and Crofters*, Edinburgh 1982.

SIMPSON, Myrtle *'Skisters': the Story of Scottish Skiing*, Carrbridge 1982.

SMITH, David B *Curling: an Illustrated History*, Edinburgh 1981.

There are general histories which have material on Scotland which is not easily found elsewhere:

HAYES, Alfred H *The Story of Bowls*, London 1972.

HENDERSON, Ian T, and STIRK, David I *Golf in the Making* 2nd edn, London 1982.

There are good books on sport in Britain which give a setting for its history in Scotland, including:

BRAILSFORD, Denis *Sport, Time and Society: the British at Play*, London 1991.

BRAILSFORD, Denis *British Sport - a Social History*, Cambridge 1992.

HOLT, Richard *Sport and the British*, Oxford 1989.

On the enjoyment of sport:

BORTHWICK, Alastair *Always a Little Further*, Stirling 1939.

MACVICAR, Angus *Golf in my Gallowses*, London 1983.

MURRAY, W H *Mountaineering in Scotland*, London 1947.

Scotland has produced one fine novel about football:

JENKINS, Robin *The Thistle and the Grail*, Edinburgh 1954.

Although in general this list omits histories of clubs - hundreds have been written - one must be mentioned which gives a human picture of the links between the growth and decline of a community and its football team:

FERGUSON, Ronald *Black Diamonds and the Blue Brazil: a History of Coal, Cowdenbeath and Football*, Ellon 1993.

There is an extensive list of club histories in:

COX, Richard William *Sport in Britain: a Bibliography of Historical Publications*, Manchester 1991.